HOW TO WRITE

A KILLER ACT ESSAY

TOM CLEMENTS

HIT 'EM UP PUBLISHING

CALIFORNIA 2014

TC TUTORING "Making Students Smarter, One Step at a Time" www.tctutoring.net / tctutoring@comcast.net

TC TUTORING
346 Rheem Blvd, Suite 110-B
Moraga, California, 94556
www.tctutoring.net

First Edition: January 2014

Cover design by Namita Kapoor

Special thanks to Niki, Sumi, Sachi, Suki and, of course, Michi

Printed in the United States of America
ISBN: 978-0-578-13590-8

BLURBS

TK, California
"Tom's ACT writing methodology was enormously helpful to me when preparing for the ACT essay and actually writting it during the test. The system of dividing the prompt into pro and cons using a T-chart and finding different perspectives was a huge time saver that allowed me to organize my ideas in a concise manner so I could easily incorporate them into the essay. With Tom's help, I went into the essay with confidence, I finished with 5 minutes to spare, and I scored a 12."

MS, California
"Tom's T-chart method helped me fully understand how to compare and contrast ideas on a central topic effectively, how to transition fluidly from one point to another, and how to cohesively knit together an argument that not only takes a firm stance but also has a great level of sophistication. He makes the daunting process of facing a timed essay seem doable and now it is the easiest part of the test for me."

BM, California
"Tom Clements' "How To Write A Killer ACT Essay" was definitely the number one help in my process for studying for the ACT. The book really simplifies the process of writing the essay and breaks it down into easy steps that anyone can follow! The T-Chart method that Tom teaches through his book is the best strategy one could use when writing an ACT essay and I'm so thankful to have learned it. When students think of writing essays, especially ones for the SAT and ACT, they tend to freak out. I was this way as well, until I read Tom's book. After using his essay strategies, I literally aced my ACT essay. This book was awesome and I recommend it for anyone taking the ACT, good writers or not."

CONTEXT

"Be yourself; everyone else is already taken."
— Oscar Wilde

"Do not fear to be eccentric in opinion, for every opinion now accepted was once eccentric."
— Bertrand Russell

"People can tell you to keep your mouth shut, but that doesn't stop you from having your own opinion."
— Anne Frank, *The Diary of a Young Girl*

"You must look within for value, but must look beyond for perspective."
— Denis Waitley

"Everything we hear is an opinion, not a fact. Everything we see is a perspective, not the truth."
— Marcus Aurelius, *Meditations*

Table of Contents

1—Introduction

As a prospective ACT test taker — or the parent of a test taker or a professional ACT tutor — the first question you should ask yourself when debating the purchase of a manual is this: Why should I buy this book? How does it differ from other ACT books on the market? Well, OK, that's two questions but they're equally valid. Here's why:

- Most ACT manuals try to cover *everything* on the test, paying only cursory attention to the essay. This book deals *only* with the essay and provides a clear and comprehensive methodology that any student can use to quickly compose a top-scoring essay.

- As part of this methodology, visual reference points in the form of T-charts are provided to help you parse the prompt — the ACT topic — quickly and confidently into pro and con arguments, around which you can organize your essay.

- Real essays from real students are provided, offering you dramatic insight into how the simple tips described in this book have been put into actual practice in top-scoring essays.

- If you are an SAT student looking to hedge your bets for college admission by taking the ACT, an extra chapter is provided to help you apply SAT techniques to ACT prompts.

In a minute, we'll delve into parsing the prompt and describing the methodology behind top-scoring essays. But first, just so you know what you're getting into, a few words on the general structure of the ACT are in order.

ACT Structure

The ACT is comprised of five parts: Writing, Math, Reading, the dreaded Science section and the thirty-minute essay. Although the essay is presented as an *optional* part of the test, many schools refuse to recognize ACT scores unless accompanied by the essay. If you are absolutely certain that the only colleges and universities on your academic dance card are those that don't require the essay, then you don't need this book. For the rest of you, the essay is mandatory. Better safe than sorry.

≡
___

Unlike the SAT, where test sections are interleaved so that students have to shift repeatedly between subject matter, the ACT is a more focused (and kinder, gentler) test which presents each subject matter section once and only once. As a result, students can concentrate fully on Writing (mainly grammar), followed by Math, then Reading, then Science, and finally the "optional" ACT Essay.

- Writing

  Grammar — Four short narratives presented, 75 questions posed and a total of 45 minutes provided. See chapter 6 for an overview of ACT grammar tips to help speed you through this section.

- Math

  Algebra, geometry, trigonometry — 60 mostly straightforward, classroom-based math question with a total of 60 minutes provided. One question per minute. Not too bad if you've paid attention in school.

- Reading

  Texts — Four types of passages presented: prose, social science, humanities and natural science, each containing 10 questions for a total of 40 questions posed in a total of 35 minutes. Ouch!

- Science

  Data — Seven passages drawn from various science areas are presented. Not so much science as data interpretation. The emphasis is placed on numeric correlation of information contained in charts, graphs and tables. 40 questions posed and a total of 35 minutes provided. Brutal!

- "Optional" Essay

  Composition — A prompt of personal relevance to high school students is presented with various pro and con positions articulated. A total of 30 minutes and four pages of lined space are provided. Piece of cake, once you get my methodology down.

The Prompt

Every ACT Essay begins with a prompt that discusses some question of relevance to high school students. Unlike the SAT Essay, whose prompts involve broad, sweeping issues that are typically handled with examples from history and literature, the ACT Essay revolves around a micro prompt, with issues touching on everyday life.

The prompt provides students with "dueling" points of view. In other words, the merits of an issue are discussed (both pro and con) and students are asked to compose a well-written essay that demonstrates their ability to navigate between these points of view. Students are expected to express their *personal opinions* by **taking a strong position on one side of the prompt**. At the same time, students are expected to demonstrate objectivity by including a so-called **concession paragraph** in their essay, arguing the merits of a contrary point of view.

Here's a sample ACT prompt with "dueling" points of view:

> In some high schools, many parents and educators have encouraged the school to adopt a dress code that sets guidelines for what students can wear in the school building. Some teachers and parents support a dress code because they think it will improve the learning environment in the school. Other teachers and parents do not support a dress code because they think it restricts individual freedom of expression. In your opinion, should high schools adopt a dress code for students?

> In your essay, take a position on this question. You may write about either one of the two points of view given, or you may present a different point of view on this question. Use specific reasons and examples to support your position.

Right away you can see lines being drawn between supporters of a learning environment and champions of freedom of expression. Lines drawn between those who think current fashion is distracting and want to prohibit it and those who think individuals should be free to make their own fashion statement.

Students must navigate between these conflicting points of view in their essays and present their own *opinions* backed by supporting details. At first, this may seem like a daunting proposition. But don't worry, using the T-chart technique described in the following chapters, you'll be able to parse the prompt quickly into *pros* and *cons*, choose a preferred position, and get off to a jump-start on your essay.

Keep in mind that all ACT prompts revolve around matters of *opinion*. They all deal with local situations high school students can or should have an intelligent opinion on. And they all require you to evaluate BOTH sides of an issue WHILE taking a strong stand on one side or the other.

To get a better idea of the types of questions students are likely to encounter as ACT prompts, here are a few more sample prompts, boiled down to their bare essentials:

- Should teenagers be required to maintain a "C" average in school before receiving a driver's license?

- Should high school be extended to five years?
- Should high school students have an active role in classroom instruction?
- Should businesses and factories located near schools be required to eliminate the pollutants and harmful emissions they release into the air?
- Should high schools require students to complete a certain number of hours of community service?

As you can probably deduce from these examples, all ACT prompts revolve around control issues where someone in a position of authority wants to control some school-based activity of teenagers.

The basic paradigm of the ACT prompt is thus distilled in the following table:

In all ACT prompts some . . .		
parent		impose
teacher		mandate	some school-
school administrator	WANTS TO	block	related
government official		require	activity of
community member		restrict	teenagers

Your job is to process the information in the prompt, break it down into pro and con positions, take a strong stand on the side you think merits the most support, and get your pencil moving. You've got a total of 30 minutes to get this job done.

White Space

Once you've been presented with the prompt, you're provided with four pages of white space to generate your essay.

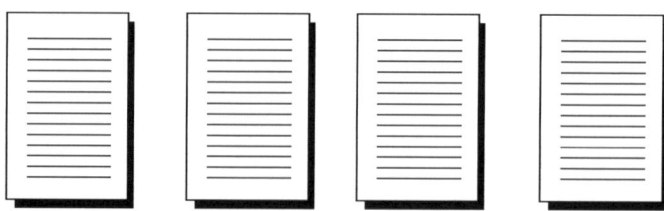

Four pages of white space

Although four pages are provided, it's not necessary to fill them all. However, to obtain a top score from the ACT Readers, you must fill in *at least two* of the pages completely and, *preferably, some portion of the third*. The point, really, is to fill up enough white space to equal **at least 450 words**. Filling all four pages is possible only if you have a robotic arm and the ability to trance-channel Jack Kerouac.

Top-scoring essays are invariably judged as much by length as by persuasive prose.

ACT Readers — Who are These People?

The ACT recruits high school and college teachers (typically, English teachers) to grade your essay, giving it a score from "1" to "6". Since two Readers are assigned to each essay, the top composite score is "12".

Because the essay is "optional", your score is included as a separate entry with your ACT results. The essay, consequently, has no bearing on the Writing portion of your ACT.

At some point after the test has been scored, your essay, along with thousands of others, is scanned by a computer, turned into a PDF file and downloaded to an ACT database for eventual distribution to selected Readers.

Each Reader receives a batch of essays and begins the scoring process. But don't expect the Readers to grade your essay as a high school teacher might. No surplus of red ink, no meticulous attention to detail.

Readers get paid by the hour and the more essays they grade, the more chance they have of being invited back to participate in future essay-grading marathons. Therefore, the incentive for the Reader is to move through each essay as swiftly as possible, spending no more than 2 minutes per essay.

That's right. Your Reader takes a leisurely stroll down essay lane, grading your prose in less than 10% of the time it took you to write it.

On the surface, this may seem twisted and unfair, but you can make it work to your advantage. Knowing ACT Readers prefer to work fast, you can structure your essay to help them do just that.

Two things are essential in this regard. You must:

- Make a good first impression with your opening paragraph. To do this, present not just your own opinion but the opinions of others, which, thankfully, the ACT will provide you on a silver platter.

- Use clear transitions throughout your essay so that the Reader can follow, Oz-like, the yellow-brick writing road.

What's Next

In the next chapter, we'll take a look at the criteria employed by Readers to judge your essay, which, not coincidentally, correspond to criteria for good writing in general.

2—Rules of Engagement

As Marcus Aurelius pointed out two millennia ago, "Everything we hear is an **opinion**, not a fact. Everything we see is a **perspective**, not the truth."

Both soldier and philosopher, Marcus Aurelius was way ahead of his time when it comes to planning for the ACT Essay since, strictly speaking, the essay is really just a matter of opinion.

Not *just* your opinion but the opinions of others, which, thankfully, the ACT serves up on a silver platter for you to choose from at the beginning of each essay. How is this so? The ACT incorporates into its essay prompt — the topic it expects you to write about — multiple points of view which you can draw from and expand on when composing your essay.

In some sense, this makes the job of ACT essay writing easier than that of SAT writing, where you're expected to hold forth on subject matter you yourself bring to the table. The ACT, in other words, gives you both an organizational boost and a head start on composing your thoughts and marshalling your arguments — both pro and con — before your composition work even begins.

Once you use the prompt to develop the comparisons and contrasts you want to present to the ACT reader and choose the side you want to support, then it's just a matter of implementing some simple *Rules of Engagement* to ensure a top-scoring essay. These rules are presented in this chapter as a complete writing methodology that has proven successful for hundreds of my former students.

These rules, it turns out, mirror the rules employed by readers to judge your essay, which, not coincidentally, correspond to the criteria for good writing in general.

Rules of Engagement — Seven Criteria

There are seven commonly-agreed upon criteria for judging good writing. Collectively these comprise a rubric, or a set of rules, employed as an ACT scoring guide. These include:

- Introduction

Your intro paragraph must have a clearly defined topic sentence or thesis. Moreover, your introduction must include multiple points of view, both pro and con, to demonstrate your ability to look at all sides of an issue. The ACT essay is a comparison and contrast essay.

- Structure

  Your essay must follow the classic five to seven paragraph format; that is, an introductory paragraph, three to five body paragraphs, and a conclusion. Because the ACT essay demands comparison and contrast, you can use multiple body paragraphs to shift between conflicting points of view.

- Transitions

  Your essay must have smooth transitions both *between* paragraphs and *within* paragraphs. Intelligent transitions, the mark of a good writer in general, are particularly important on the ACT essay, where pro and con positions on the prompt must be clearly delineated.

  A detailed look at transitions is provided at the end of this chapter.

- Subordination

  Good prose style is characterized by heavy use of subordination. Subordination lends variety to your writing style by replacing short, choppy, subject-verb-object sentences with longer, more elegant sentences that incorporate dependent clauses.

  Subordination, in a nutshell, is a way to ensure sentence variety in your writing style. The more subordination, the more sophisticated the prose.

  A detailed look at subordination is provided at the end of this chapter.

- Flash Vocabulary

  An extensive vocabulary is the mark of a good writer. Remember that part of your job on the ACT essay is to impress the reader with your use of interesting and sophisticated vocab sprinkled throughout your essay.

- Details, Details, Details

  The devil, as they always say, is in the details. Nowhere is this more important than in ACT writing. Two reasons: first of all, you have to fill up as much white space as possible to obtain a top score; second, the more detail you provide in your essay, the more compelling the narrative.

  To avoid wishy-washy abstract writing — and a low scoring essay — put some teeth into your prose by presenting concrete descriptions with finely focused analysis. Top scoring ACT essays typically run close to 450 words. Size matters!

- Narrative Cohesion and Logical Flow

  These two go hand-in-hand. Good transitions assure logical flow and logical flow assures narrative cohesion.

  The hallmark of a top-scoring essay is not just a bunch of facts strung together in linear formation. Top scoring ACT essays exhibit a cohesive narrative flow where diverse viewpoints meld together harmoniously and a strong common thread runs throughout.

In ensuing chapters, I'll elaborate on how to incorporate these clear and simple writing principles into your essay to ensure a top score from the readers. But speaking of top scores, let's take a quick look at what the ACT considers a "6".

Remember, two readers will evaluate your essay. Receiving a "6" from each gets you a score of "12".

ACT Scoring Guidelines

The ACT scoring guidelines are available for viewing on the ACT website, so I won't reprint all of them here. If you're interested, you can find them at: http://www.act.org/

However, since students reading this book are typically striving for a top score, I'll include the ACT criteria for a "6" with its own, convoluted terminology intact.

Then I'll cut through the verbiage and compare the "official" ACT scoring rubric to the *Rules of Engagement* I just presented in plain English. Here's the official ACT text:

Score = 6

Essays within this score range demonstrate effective skill in responding to the task.

The essay shows a clear understanding of the task. The essay takes a position on the issue and may offer a critical context for discussion. The essay addresses complexity by examining different perspectives on the issue, or by evaluating the implications and/or complications of the issue, or by fully responding to counter arguments to the writer's position. Development of ideas is ample, specific, and logical. Most ideas are fully elaborated. A clear focus on the specific issue in the prompt is maintained. The organization of the essay is clear: the organization may be somewhat predictable or it may grow from the writer's purpose. Ideas are logically sequenced. Most transitions reflect the writer's logic and are usually integrated into the essay. The introduction and conclusion are effective, clear, and well developed. The essay shows a good command of language. Sentences are varied and word choice is varied and precise. There are few, if any, errors to distract the reader.

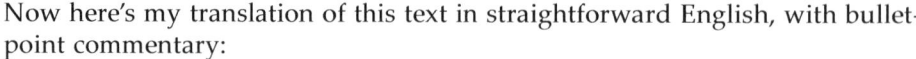

Now here's my translation of this text in straightforward English, with bullet-point commentary:

- The essay has logical transitions with a clear beginning, middle and end. Plan your essay carefully before you start to write. Chart a clear, well-organized course.

- The essay takes a strong position on the prompt and maintains a logical focus throughout. Don't ramble. Stay on target.

- The essay presents different perspectives on the prompt by addressing both pro and con arguments. Show both sides of the issue. Maintain balance.

- The essay presents arguments which are fully elaborated. No skimping on pro and con detail and no unduly abstract discussion. Be specific. The more examples cited the better. The more detail the better.

- The essay employs transitions between and within paragraphs to guide the reader in a logical fashion through the arguments presented.

- Most transitions reflect the writer's logic and are well-integrated into the essay. Use transition words to provide narrative cohesion.

- The essay shows a good command of language with varied sentence structure and good word choice. Employ subordination — sentence variety — and flash vocab throughout.

Essays receiving less than "6" are deficient in one or more of these criteria.

As you can see, the "official" ACT rubric is really just a more dense and convoluted expression of my own seven *Rules of Engagement*. Simply following the rules and methodology described in this book, ANYONE can learn to write a top-scoring ACT essay.

Transitions

Because the ACT provides prompts that provide multiple points of view, good writers need to make copious use of transitions, which allow ACT Readers to follow the narrative flow of the composition.

You see this all the time in good writing. Transition words like "consequently" and "therefore" help the reader understand the logical sequencing of the composition. Transition words like "however" and "on the other hand" are employed to emphasize a change in direction in the argument.

When grading essays, ACT readers, like all standardized test graders, prefer a guided tour through your essay; they hate unnecessary digressions and unwarranted zig-zags. They want to get through your prose as quickly as possible. You're going to spend 30 minutes pouring out your opinions — and heart and soul — in your essay; however, the readers may only spend 2 minutes scoring your essay.

Transition words, as we'll see later, can be used both *within* paragraphs and *between* paragraphs; they're like signposts on a highway, clearly delineating for the Reader the logical twists and turns in the development of your essay. Moreover, transitions are the mark of a mind that knows how to handle both sides of an argument, an attribute essential to top-scoring ACT essays.

Following is a list of common transitions, divided into those that propel the narrative forward (pro) and those that signify a counterpoint (con) or reverse direction to the argument. Keep this list in mind. In fact, you might want to circle it here and/or dog ear this page. As we'll see in the next chapter, transitions are a great complement to perspectives on the prompt.

List of Transitions

Pro	Con
consequently	however
therefore	on the other hand
along the same lines	in contrast to
in fact	ironically
furthermore	although
in addition	yet
moreover	despite
clearly	unfortunately
to ensure this	to take issue with that
on top of that	but

Subordination

Since the ACT essay is a writing test, sentence variety (subordination) is essential to a top score. Bad writers compose sentences with little narrative flow, simple subject-verb-object concoctions that don't carry much punch.

Good writers use subordination to lend variety to their writing style by replacing short, choppy, subject-verb-object sentences with longer, more elegant sentences that incorporate dependent and independent clauses.

Take the following examples of two boring subject-verb-object sentences stuck together with a period.

> Mahatma Ghandi decided on a hunger strike to fight British Colonialism. He inspired the India Independence movement.

Functional but boring. There are three different ways to rearrange and subordinate these choppy sentences to make them more interesting. For example:

- After deciding on a hunger strike to fight British Colonialism, Mahatma Ghandi inspired the India Independence movement.

  Notice the long lead-in *After deciding on a hunger strike to fight British Colonialism,* which now precedes the subject of the sentence, Mahatma Ghandi. This is a much better use of sentence variety.

- Mahatma Ghandi, an inspiration to the India Independence movement, decided on a hunger strike to fight British Colonialism.

  In this example, the inserted phrase *an inspiration to the India Independence movement* is now sandwiched, to much greater effect, between the main subject and verb of the sentence.

- Mahatma Ghandi decided on a hunger strike to fight British Colonialism, inspiring the India Independence movement.

  In this example, the tag-along to the main clause *inspiring the India Independence movement* is now placed at the end of the sentence, creating smoother sentence flow.

The key point to remember is that good writing is all about narrative flow. Without subordination, sentences sit on the page like patients tranquilized upon a table. Healthy sentences, like healthy people, need to breathe, to move, to dance, to flow. Subordination makes it so.

What's Next

In the ensuing chapters, I'll elaborate on specifics. Next up, we'll see how to use a T-chart to parse the prompt into pro and con perspectives, helping us to jump-start the essay.

3—Pros and Cons

In the previous chapter, we took a look at the Rules of Engagement — building blocks and style conventions essential to structuring an ACT essay quickly and cohesively. In this chapter, I'm going to show you how to parse the prompt using a "T chart" to separate pro and con arguments.

Parsing the prompt constitutes important "pre-work" that you need to do prior to jumping directly into your essay. You have 30 minutes to compose an ACT essay and *at least three minutes* of that should be allocated to set-up time, where you break the prompt down into sub-arguments you can organize your essay around.

Trust me, this is both an easy and essential process that will lend logic and narrative cohesion to your composition.

Students who jump right into the prompt often find their arguments swaying back and forth like drunken sailors, uncertain of their footing on the shore.

T-Chart

Engineers and draftsman use T-squares to draw parallel lines and establish right angles. In much the same manner, you can draw a "T-chart" in the ACT test booklet directly below the prompt to separate *pro* and *con* arguments

Pro	Con

A T-chart provides a handy way to organize and contrast the different viewpoints presented in the prompt; moreover, it allows you to easily augment those viewpoints with others of your own.

In this chapter we'll take a look at some common ACT prompts and demonstrate how a T-chart can be used to parse — and cherry pick! — the prompt. We'll start by returning to the prompt we saw in the first chapter.

ACT Prompt 1

In some high schools, many teachers and parents have encouraged the school to require school uniforms that students must wear to school. Some teachers and parents support school uniforms because they think their use will improve the school's learning environment. Other teachers and parents do not support requiring uniforms because they think it restricts individual freedom of expression. In your opinion, should high schools require uniforms for students?

In your essay, *take a position on this question*. You may write about either one of the two points of view given, or you may present a different point of view on this question. Use specific reasons and examples to support your position.

Strategy

Split the prompt into the pro and con arguments that you want to elaborate on in your essay. Right away, you can cherry pick two arguments directly from the prompt. For example:

Pro	Con
School uniforms improve the learning environment. **Why** —	School uniforms discourage individual freedom. **Why** —

Next, elaborate sub-arguments on each side. Since the ACT essay is simply a matter of *opinion*, this shouldn't be too hard. Just stretch your imagination and picture everyday events that might relate to the topic. One strategy, demonstrated below, is to ask yourself "Why" the pro and con arguments are worthy of support.

Pro	Con
School uniforms improve the learning environment. **Why** —	School uniforms discourage individual freedom. **Why** —

Sub-arguments

They take the emphasis off fashion and onto learning	They reduce individual creativity and lead to a uniform mind set
Distractions due to provocative clothing are eliminated	Uniforms fail to prepare students for the real world where people learn to "dress for success"
Uniforms reduce income-based schoolyard bullying and "elitism"	Telling students what to wear creates a "nanny" state in high school
Uniforms put the emphasis on democratic principles and cultural equality	
They reduce the costs and effort incurred in "keeping up with the Kardashians"	

Once you've parsed the prompt into sub-arguments, determine which side of the issue makes the most sense to support. A useful strategy for doing this is to view the prompt through a series of perspectives.

Perspectives

Perspectives are a quick and surefire way to list the various points of view you want to consider when evaluating the prompt. Moreover, they are a great way to organize and introduce your body paragraphs.

There are a wide variety of perspectives to play around with. I'll present a general list below and highlight several that have a direct bearing on the prompt under consideration. For example:

- From a **financial** perspective . . .

- From a fashion perspective . . .
- From a personal perspective . . .
- From an **academic** perspective . . .
- From a psychological perspective . . .
- From a practical perspective . . .
- From a peer-group perspective . . .
- From a sports perspective . . .
- From an **egalitarian** perspective . . .
- From a pop culture perspective . . .
- From a constitutional perspective . . .
- From a health or public health perspective . . .
- From a community perspective . . .
- From a technology perspective . . .
- From a free speech perspective . . .
- From a civil liberties perspective . . .
- From a **big government** perspective . . .

Of course, there are many more that you can come up with on your own but this list should be enough to get you started. Consider how some of the sub-arguments (opinions) in the previous T-chart readily align to various perspectives:

Sub-argument	Perspective
They take the emphasis off fashion and onto learning	From an **academic** perspective . . .
Uniforms put the emphasis on democratic principles and cultural equality	From an **egalitarian** perspective . . .
They reduce the costs and effort incurred in "keeping up with the Kardashians"	From a **financial** perspective . . .
Telling students what to wear creates a "nanny" state in high school	From a **big-government** perspective . . .

Perspectives are the secret to success on the ACT essay. They help you quickly enumerate points of view around which your essay can be organized. Equally important, as can be seen in the previous table, perspectives can be used as transitions between paragraphs to smooth the flow of your presentation and clarify the logic.

Once you've constructed your T-chart, enumerated your sub-arguments, selected your perspectives, and determined which side of the prompt you want to support, you're ready to compose your introductory paragraph.

Sample Introduction

Ideally, your intro paragraph should start by establishing context with a broad, sweeping statement that defines the territory your essay will explore. You can then use your T-chart sub-arguments to weave between the multiple points of view presented in the prompt. Usually, but not necessarily, you'll want to reveal which position you plan to support in your intro. Here's how it's done:

> With the world undergoing change at an alarming rate, it is important for our schools to provide a safe and efficient learning environment for students. To ensure this, many teachers and parents have encouraged schools to require school uniforms because they think their use will improve the school's learning environment. *However,* other teachers and parents disagree, arguing that uniforms restrict individual freedom of expression. Citing fears of an encroaching "nanny state", these educators feel school districts should not unnecessarily burden students with non-academic restrictions. *On the other hand,* a school system with no rules in place for appropriate dress may result in a fashion free-for-all, where students with the most money flaunt their wealth and look down on less affluent students. *Clearly,* this approach flies in the face of the democratic principles that schools are supposed to uphold and encourage. *Consequently,* school uniforms, both less costly and more egalitarian, promote the best learning environment for high school students.

Most people — in fact, most writers — have a hard time getting started. Students in particular are antsy; their tendency is to just jump into the essay and start writing, often haphazardly. However, taking a few minutes to draw up a T-chart to formulate your arguments lets you hit the ground running when you begin your essay.

Instead of starting completely from scratch, you wisely make use of the material the ACT has so helpfully provided you in the prompt, augmented by your own opinions and perspectives. Doing so provides you — and the ACT Reader — with a logical roadmap that ensures a well-organized and top-scoring essay.

═
───

While expressing multiple points of view in your intro, keep in mind the position you eventually want to support. You can either conclude your intro by taking a firm position on the prompt — as demonstrated in the sample above — or you can wait for your body paragraphs to do so.

Finally, notice how this introduction employs liberal use of transitions to navigate the various points of view in the intro:

- *however*
- *on the other hand*
- *clearly*
- *consequently*

As I mentioned in the previous chapter, transitions are the mark of a good writer. While perspectives provide a quick and useful way to organize your arguments, transitions clarify the logic of your composition and smooth the narrative flow. It's not an exaggeration to say they are the literary super-glue that holds a top-scoring composition together. Make them your friend.

Summary

Here are the key things to keep in mind when composing an introduction:

- Use a broad, sweeping statement to open the intro and establish context for the prompt
- State the pro and con positions from your T-chart, mixing in a generous helping of sub-arguments
- Use transition words to move back and forth between various points of view
- Add in any details that help to flesh out the presentation
- Optionally, take a strong stand on one side of the argument

Sample Body Paragraphs

Unlike the introduction, where multiple points of view are presented, body paragraphs encapsulate individual points. In each body paragraph, writers should:

- Take a strong position on some part of the prompt
- Qualify that position with perspectives
- Add interesting details (details, details) to flesh out the presentation
- Wrap things up and move on to your next point

To demonstrate this process, here are two body paragraphs from a sample essay on the "high school uniform" prompt written by one of my students that highlight the use of perspectives in an ACT essay.

Body paragraph 1

> *From a financial perspective,* having school uniforms would relieve me of the need to "shop till I drop" at the nearest mall. The money I save on clothes could be more productively spent at my local bookstore, catching up on trash novels like "The Hunger Games" or re-reading classics from my freshman year like "To Kill a Mockingbird" or "Wuthering Heights", my personal favorite.

Body paragraph 2

> *From a peer-group perspective,* I would welcome the reduction in stress and tension that invariably occurs when girls comment negatively on each other's outfits. It's not nice to say so but girls can sometimes be "catty". School uniforms would level the playing field between the "in group" and those less blessed with innate fashion sense. This latter group, I have to admit, sometimes includes me!

A word of caution here. I'm not advocating that you start *every* body paragraph with a "From the perspective of . . . " phrase — that would be too formulaic and repetitive. But using perspectives as an organizing principle and interspersing them in strategic points throughout the essay is a surefire recipe for success.

In some sense, parsing the prompt for sub-arguments and enumerating perspectives entails a chicken and the egg scenario. Which comes first —brainstorming sub-argument opinions or considering perspectives? The answer is simple; they work hand in hand and are both pragmatic shortcuts to help you quickly come up with content examples for your essay.

Every essay should have an introduction, four to five body paragraphs (depending on length) and a conclusion.

The conclusion is actually the easiest part of your essay; you just sum up the points you've made previously and add a concluding flourish, which we'll see in the sample essay in the next chapter. Stay tuned.

For now, having seen the strategies required to analyze one ACT prompt, let's take a look at a second, constructing another T-chart to parse the prompt.

ACT Prompt 2

> Educators debate extending high school to five years because of increasing demands on students from employers and colleges to participate in extracurricular activities and community service in addition to having high grades. Some educators support extending high school to five years because they think students need more time to achieve all that is expected of them. Other educators do not support extending high school to five years because

they think students would lose interest in school and attendance would drop in the fifth year. In your opinion, should high school be extended to five years?

In your essay, take a position on this question. You may write about either one of the two points of view given, or you may present a different point of view on this question. Use specific reasons and examples to support your position.

Strategy

As before, split the prompt into the pro and con arguments that you want to elaborate on in your essay. Again, right away, you can cherry pick two arguments directly from the prompt. For example:

Pro	Con
High school should be extended to five years. **Why** —	High school should not be extended to five years. **Why** —

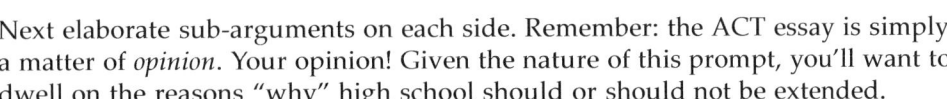

Next elaborate sub-arguments on each side. Remember: the ACT essay is simply a matter of *opinion*. Your opinion! Given the nature of this prompt, you'll want to dwell on the reasons "why" high school should or should not be extended.

Pro	Con
High school should be extended to five years. **Why** —	High school should not be extended to five years. **Why** —

Sub-arguments

Due to increased demand for extracurricular activities like sports	Because students would lose interest in school and drop out
To provide more time for volunteer work	Because schools would lose federal funds if the student population declines
To provide more time to devote to difficult coursework such as AP and science classes	Because many students go on to graduate school and adding one more year to high school is counterproductive
Helps make students more likely to succeed in college	Because this represents an unnecessary intrusion of big government into local school districts

Once you've established your pro and con arguments, you can align them with perspectives.

Perspectives

Sub-argument	Perspective
Due to increasing demands for extracurricular activities like sports	From an **athletic** perspective...
To provide more time to devote to difficult coursework such as AP and science classes	From an **academic** perspective...
To provide more time for volunteer work	From a **community** perspective...
Because schools would lose federal funds if the student population declines	From a **financial** perspective...
Because students would lose interest in school and drop out	From a **personal** perspective...

These perspectives can then be used to organize your essay and/or to populate your paragraphs.

Sample Body Paragraphs

Here are two sample paragraphs from different students on "extending high school to five years". The first embeds the perspective at the end of the paragraph; the other uses perspective as a transition.

Body paragraph 1

> Sports have always been an intrinsic part of my academic life. Sitting in a classroom, while productive in terms of knowledge gained, is not conducive to overall health. In a world dominated by digital devices and online gaming, teenagers today need to keep active in order to stay healthy. The obesity epidemic is already threatening many adolescents with early-onset diabetes and metabolic syndrome. On top of that, physical education has declined in our nation's primary schools. *From a health and athletic perspective*, being able to devote more time to sports during a fifth year of high school might be just what the doctor ordered.

Body paragraph 2

> *From a financial perspective*, extending high school to five years would pose significant funding problems for high school administrators, especially those responsible for inner city schools where the dropout rate is already high. Federal funding is tied directly to student population. The more students a school has the more federal dollars it has at its disposal. If, as many experts argue, extending high school to five years results in an increase in high school dropouts, our already underfunded inner city schools would suffer disproportionately. This could be considered a form of financial discrimination. The Supreme Court decision in "Brown vs Board of Education" in the early fifties made it clear that laws establishing separate schools for black and white students were unconstitutional. Do we really want to go back to the days of "separate but equal"? Extending high school to five years might result in just that.

Both of these body paragraphs augment the writer's opinions by bringing in cultural and historical references, an excellent way to ensure a top-scoring essay. The first paragraph mentions the obesity epidemic and brings in a technical reference to "metabolic syndrome". The second puts the argument in historical context by referencing one the most significant Supreme Court decisions of the 20th century.

Bringing in outside material like this to buttress your arguments is key to top-scoring essays. Opinions can be expressed much more forcefully when objective material (historic, literary, scientific, sociological, etc.) is brought in for support.

ACT Prompt 3

Finally, one last prompt to consider. At this point, you might feel comfortable enough with the strategies I've presented to parse the prompt yourself.

Try it on your own by first reading the next prompt and then constructing a quick T-chart in the margins with pro and con arguments. Then come up with your own sub-arguments for each side before moving on to the Strategy section, where several approaches are broached.

I'll leave it to you as an exercise to come up with your own sample paragraphs based on your T-chart. But don't worry. If you're not quite up to that task yet, just proceed on to the next chapter where a complete sample essay awaits you.

> In some states, legislators have debated whether teenagers should be required to maintain a "C" grade average in school before receiving a driver's license. Some people think this would be a good policy because having passing grades shows that students are responsible enough to be good drivers. Other people think such a policy would not be appropriate because they see no

relationship between grades in school and driving skills. In your opinion, should teenagers be required to maintain a "C" average in school before receiving a driver's license?

In your essay, take a position on this question. You may write about either one of the two points of view given, or you may present a different point of view on this question. Use specific reasons and examples to support your position.

Strategy

Once again, split the prompt into the pro and con opinions and elaborate your sub-arguments.

Pro	Con
Teenagers should be required to maintain a "C" average before receiving a driver's licence. **Why —**	Teenagers should *not* be required to maintain a "C" average before receiving a driver's licence. **Why —**

Sub-arguments

Students with good grades are responsible drivers	No relationship between grades and driving
Driving is a privilege not a right	Driving is necessary for many students to get to and from school and work
Teenage roadside fatalities have increased due to poor drivers	Withholding driver's licences would unfairly discriminate among poor students
	Such mandates represent an unnecessary intrusion of big government into local school district affairs

Next tag each sub-argument with perspectives.

Perspectives

Sub-argument	Perspective
Driving is necessary for many students to get to and from school and work	From a **practical** perspective . . .
Withholding driver's licences would unfairly discriminate among poor students	From a **constitutional** perspective . . .
Teenage roadside fatalities have increased due to poor drivers	From a **public health** perspective . . .

Overview

For students who want a quick overview of the methodology described in this and previous chapters, the key points so far are these:

- Use a T-chart to parse the prompt into pro and con positions and generate sub-arguments for these positions.
- Write an introduction that establishes context for your essay and summarizes the multiple points of view contained in your T-chart.
- Compose body paragraphs based on the sub-arguments in your T-chart, using perspectives to organize your presentation and, at times, provide transitions between/within paragraphs. When constructing arguments, add as much detail as possible.
- For top-scoring essays, the devil is always in the details. Use objective material — supreme court cases, constitutional issues, environmental restrictions — to support your opinions and arguments.
- Make liberal use of transitions within and between paragraphs to help the reader understand the logic of your presentation and appreciate the narrative flow.
- Keep your sentence structure varied. Avoid choppy subject-verb-object sentences. Use subordination (independent phrases and clauses) to create a more sophisticated writing style.
- Remember to keep your pencil moving. Word count matters. Top-scoring ACT essays usually run at least 450 words.

Throughout all of this, because your opinions are your own, you are free to come up with whatever arguments or counter-arguments seem feasible. As Marcus Aurelius said in the opening passage of the previous chapter:

≡

"Everything we hear is a matter of opinion . . . everything we see is a perspective."

What's Next

In the following chapter, we'll pull all these threads together and review a complete sample essay.

4—Sample Essay

Before you begin writing, spend three or four minutes to analyze the prompt box. As we've seen in previous chapters, the ACT actually helps you get started on your essay by suggesting various points of views.

Remember: the ACT is all about opinions and perspectives. In sports, good teams take advantage of what the defense has to offer. The ACT offers you several different points of view. Use these viewpoints to construct a T-chart.

Here's the prompt from the June 2013 ACT test. In this chapter, we'll parse the prompt, marshall sub-arguments, add perspectives and construct a sample essay based on our analysis.

ACT Prompt — June 2013

Educators debate whether high school students should have an active role in classroom instruction, such as selecting some course materials and leading some class discussions. Some educators support giving students an active role in classroom instruction because they think doing so would increase students' interest in their classes. Other educators do not support giving students an active role in classroom instruction because they think students would not learn as much from their peers as they would from a teacher. In your opinion, should high school students have an active role in classroom instruction?

In your essay, take a position on this question. You may write about either one of the two points of view given, or you may present a different point of view on this question. Use specific reasons and examples to support your position.

Cherry Pick the Prompt

The first order of business is to split the prompt into the pro and con arguments presented to you by the ACT. You'll want to elaborate on those in your essay, but right away you can cherry pick two arguments directly from the prompt and bank off of them to elaborate sub-arguments. For example:

Pro	Con
Student teachers should have an active role in the classroom. **Why** —	Student teachers should not have an active role in the classroom. **Why** —

Sub-arguments

They provide an alternate perspective on the subject	They take away time from professional teachers who are more qualified
They make learning more relevant and fun	Classroom decorum is disrupted
They foster an easy-going classroom atmosphere which helps reduce stress	
They benefit from better presentation abilities	

This parsing of the prompt should take you 3, no more than 4, minutes. Having accomplished that, you're now armed and dangerous and ready to write. You've got opinions. You've mapped out your arguments. All you need are a few perspectives.

Perspectives

From the previous chapter, recall that perspective can act as both transitions between paragraphs and organizing principles around which you can construct your essay. Perspectives, therefore, are both a literary tool and a way to reinforce your T-chart arguments. Here's a quick recap of the main perspectives:

- From a financial perspective . . .
- From an academic perspective . . .
- From a personal perspective . . .
- From a **psychological** perspective . . .
- From an egalitarian perspective . . .
- From a practical perspective . . .
- From a **peer-group** perspective . . .

- From a sports perspective . . .
- From a pop culture perspective . . .
- From a constitutional perspective . . .
- From a free speech perspective . . .
- From a civil liberty perspective . . .
- From a big government perspective . . .
- From a health perspective . . .

In the following sample essay, two of these have been employed to enhance the argument:

- From a **psychological** perspective . . .
- From a **peer-group** perspective . . .

As a general rule, you can employ these as transitions between paragraphs or, more subtly, weave them within paragraphs to make your point.

But remember: you don't want to over-use these perspectives and imbalance your essay. Think of them as seasonings you might add to a dish to enhance — but not overwhelm — the flavor.

To construct your introduction, start with a broad, sweeping statement that establishes the context for your essay. Then, using transition words and phrases, weave between the arguments, describing both pro and con positions. Finally, either take a stand, siding with one position over another, or leave your view open-ended, to be elaborated on in a later paragraph.

Sample Essay

With education more crucial than ever for the future success of our nation, it is important to have as streamlined an educational system as possible. The idea that students should play a role in helping to instruct their peers in the classroom is currently a debated topic. On one hand, the new perspective on a subject a student could provide may help others grasp certain information better. On the other hand, most people would agree that a teacher is more qualified to assess educational issues. Those in opposition to letting students have a hand in instruction argue that teachers should be the only ones allowed to teach. Still, having students teach their peers could not only help academically but could also foster an easygoing classroom setting to help reduce stress.

From a peer-group perspective, one of the main benefits of students taking an active role in the learning process is the fresh, alternative perspective they would bring to the subject matter. Often, students may not see eye to eye with their instructors. Having their peers make presentations on various subjects could fill in some gaps for students in their overall understanding of academic material.

Additionally, having students occasionally teach lessons would provide a much-needed change of pace for the whole class. The unending repetition of having one teacher give lectures or presentations every day can get very monotonous. If a student were to prepare his or her own lectures, the refreshing style of a new peer-group instructor would revive interest and further engage the class. Sometimes a lighter and more relevant presentation is exactly what students need to make classes more enjoyable and learning more fun.

While the idea of having students teach their own peers is clearly quite appealing, it does not come without complications. Those who oppose this idea argue that since teachers are well qualified and have all the required credentials, they are the ones who can best teach the class since they possess a Bachelor or Master degree. Moreover, having unqualified students teaching the class could prove disruptive and counter-productive.

On the other hand, older teachers, especially those who are set in their ways and teach the same subject the same way for many years, sometimes lose interest themselves in the subject matter. It would be a breath of fresh air for students and perhaps professionally motivating for teachers to see how different students present the same material. Teachers could even grade student presentations and reward students with extra credit points for the best presentations.

Of course, opponents to this course of action might argue that not all students would be comfortable with the responsibility of having to instruct the class. I disagree. **From a psychological perspective**, such an experience could well help alleviate their anxiety and improve their public speaking ability. After all, if you don't face your fears, you will never overcome them.

In sum, the idea of a system where pupils help in teaching their classmates is highly appealing. Not only would it ease the current strain of repetition in school, it would also assist in making information more accessible and relevant to students. After working out a few kinks, we could utilize this system to improve the status quo in education.

So there you have it. A complete ACT essay from start to finish. Now, to pull back the curtain and see what's really going on inside, the next section breaks this essay down into the component parts that went into its construction.

Note: This is a sample essay. A real essay from a real student on the same subject matter is provided in Chapter 4.

Building Blocks

Every ACT essay is really just a series of building blocks stacked one on top of the other. One of the tricks to writing an essay in thirty minutes or less is knowing how to assemble these blocks quickly into a cohesive whole.

In this section, we walk through the sample essay from start to finish, highlighting the function of each of the major building blocks and showing, with snippets from the essay, how that function is put into play.

In other words, notice how:

- The introduction of the essay sets the scene by simply repeating the topic and stating the pros and cons virtually verbatim from the prompt box. In other words, you don't have to come up with a provocative and original opening for the ACT. You just cherry pick the prompt.

  Of course, if you have a snappy quote or appropriate anecdote to throw at the prompt, please, be my guest. But any student can get off to a great start on the ACT essay simply by summarizing the main points discussed in the prompt box.

  Just be sure to devote sufficient attention to both sides. The easiest way to do this is to employ literary transitions that allow you to go "back and forth". In the sample essay, the following transitions (in bold) are put to good use in the intro:

  > **On one hand**, the new perspective on a subject a student could provide may help others grasp certain information better. **On the other hand**, most people would agree that a teacher is more qualified to assess educational issues.

  At the end of the intro, you may want to state the position you want to support. Although this isn't mandatory, it's a good way to establish the direction your essay is headed and prepare the Reader for the body paragraphs that follow.

  > **Still**, having students teach their peers could not only help academically but could also foster an easygoing classroom setting to help reduce stress.

  Note: It's also possible to put off taking sides in your introduction, using the first body paragraph, rather than the intro, to state your opinion on the prompt.

- The first body paragraph of the sample essay uses the "From the perspective of . . . " strategy to excellent effect.

  > **From a peer-group perspective**, one of the main benefits of students taking part in the learning process is the fresh, alternative perspective they would bring to the subject matter.

This point is then embellished with *opinions* of the author regarding ways in which student teachers could augment and enhance the academic material used in the classroom.

- The second body paragraph continues this line of thought and adds additional *opinions* regarding the positive effects of "change of pace" and ways to make "learning more fun". It's important to note that these are just opinions of the author. They may or may not be true. What's important is that they address and support the author's position.

One of the most important things to understand when constructing an ACT essay is that EVERYTHING is a matter of opinion. Your opinion, whatever it may be, is just as valid and important as something derived directly from a textbook or encyclopedia.

To return to the quote from Marcus Aurelius: "Everything we hear is an opinion, not a fact. Everything we see is a perspective, not the truth."

Your job is to come up with cogent opinions and whatever facts you can muster to support your position on the prompt.

- The third body paragraph presents a counter-argument to prompt, which the author initiates like this:

> While the idea of having students teach their own peers is clearly quite appealing, it does not come without complications.

This introduces the **CONCESSION PARAGRAPH**, which is essential to top-scoring essays since it shows the ACT readers that you are conversant with both sides of an issue and can present arguments from multiple points of view. After stating various *opinions* regarding the drawbacks of student teachers in the classroom, the author sums up the concession paragraph with this remark.

> **Moreover**, having unqualified students teaching the class could prove disruptive and counter-productive.

- In the fourth paragraph, the narrative segues from the concession paragraph back to the benefits of student teachers, concluding with the suggestion that:

> Teachers could even grade student presentations and reward students with extra credit points for the best presentations.

- With the concession paragraph out of the way, the author steps directly into the passage to tell the ACT readers "I disagree." Since the ACT essay is really just a matter of opinion, this "personal touch" represents an interesting stylistic device.

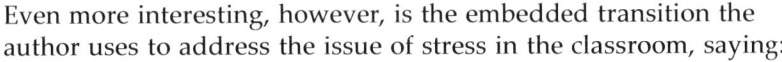

Even more interesting, however, is the embedded transition the author uses to address the issue of stress in the classroom, saying:

> **From a psychological perspective**, such an experience could well help alleviate their anxiety and improve their public speaking ability.

The paragraph concludes with a homespun homily to reinforce the "personal touch".

> After all, if you don't face your fears, you will never overcome them.

You don't have to *be* a psychologist in order to argue like one!

- The conclusion closes the sale with a general statement supporting the main position taken on the prompt.

> In sum, the idea of a system where pupils help in teaching their classmates is highly appealing. Not only would it ease the current strain of repetition in school, it would also assist in making information more accessible and relevant to students. After working out a few kinks, we could utilize this system to improve the status quo in education.

This paragraph is perhaps the easiest of the essay since it simply summarizes your position and reiterates supporting points.

Chapter Overview

Here's a recap on the main points of this chapter:

- Construct a T-chart to parse the prompt into generic *pro* and *con* arguments
- Use *perspectives* and *opinions* to generate sub-arguments
- Provide an introduction that summarizes the major issues and optionally takes a definitive position pro or con
- Compose body paragraphs that flesh out your opinions and arguments with details, details, details
- Make sure to include a concession paragraph or statement
- Employ transitions both between and within paragraphs to help organize the essay and produce a smooth and logical narrative flow
- Generate a conclusion which summarizes the points presented and makes a compelling case for your main argument

What's Next

In the following chapters, we'll expand on this theme by presenting several real essays from real students who have dominated the ACT.

One of the key features of this book — and of my overall teaching methodology — is to use real-world essays to get you up and running as a successful ACT essay writer in the shortest possible amount of time.

5—Real Essays

OK, sit back, relax — we're done with the fundamentals. We've analyzed and categorized the strategies that help you evaluate the prompt and construct a successful ACT essay.

Now let's look at some real-world essays from real-world students to see how they applied these principles and techniques to obtain high-scoring actual ACT essays.

To get things started, here's a prompt from the April, 2013 ACT. As usual, the prompt presents diverse views on a topic of some relevance to the lives of high school students and asks for your personal opinion.

ACT Prompt — April, 2013

Lawmakers debate whether businesses and factories located near schools should be required to eliminate the pollutants and harmful emissions they release into the air. Some lawmakers support such a requirement because they think schools' learning environment should include safe and healthy air for students to breathe. Other lawmakers do not support such a requirement because they think it would force businesses and factories located near schools to close or move, which could hurt local economies. In your opinion, should businesses and factories located near schools be required to eliminate the pollutants and harmful emissions they release into the air?

In your essay, take a position on this question. You may write about either one of the two points of view given, or you may present a different point of view on this question. Use specific reasons and examples to support your position.

As usual, the prompt provides you clearcut pro and con positions on the topic, giving you a jump start on your essay. All you have to do is make a sweeping introductory statement to give your essay some context, then repeat the opposing points of view described in the prompt.

Which is exactly what one of my star students, Tyler K, did, earning himself a perfect score in the process.

Tyler's Essay (score = 12)

The world we live in is progressing at an exponential rate.In the past 30 years, we have gone from inventing the first computer to now having smart-phones that can pinpoint the owner's precise location on this Earth. With this business and manufacturing boom, however, comes waste, specifically harmful emissions released into the air as a by-product of our advanced society. Sometimes these businesses and factories are located near schools, and some lawmakers argues that these factories and businesses should be ordered to eliminate the pollutions released into the air because the pollutants would harm the safe and healthy air that students can breathe. Other lawmakers argue that this requirement would force businesses and factories to move, thereby hurting local economies.

From a student's perspective, businesses and factories should eliminate pollutants from the air. School is a time when a student must always be healthy and need to learn, otherwise they may fall behind. Pollutants in the air would seriously harm student health, and may even lead to breathing problems which would then directly lead to that student not performing in school as well as they should. At my school, we have no factories or businesses remotely close to the schools, only hills full of ads on fences, and a friendly suburban neighborhood. It is quite refreshing to go outside and inhale a deep breath of cool, clean air. Also, I swim and play water polo, and from my experiences playing water polo and swimming in the polluted air of Ontario, California takes a serious toll on my lungs.

At the end of the weekend I am left wheezing and in pain from the bad air. Polluted air is the last thing our students need if they are trying to excel in school, and limiting the pollutants released by factories and businesses would be conducive to a student's well being.

From a community perspective, nearby neighborhoods would not like factories and businesses releasing harmful emissions into the air. Families would be deterred from going on Sunday walks around the block, or hosting outdoor parties in the summer time. For families with young children, the polluted air could be detrimental to their children's development as well.

Of course, simply wishing this problem away will not solve the problem. It is possible that by requiring businesses and factories to eliminate this pollution near schools, they may close or move, which would hurt the local economy. There are, however, solutions to this problem. We are at the pinnacle of alternate energy developments, and if these businesses or factories install new technology in alternative energy, they could greatly reduce their harmful emissions. Changes could be made such as installing solar panels on a building's roof, or installing LED light bulbs that use a significantly less

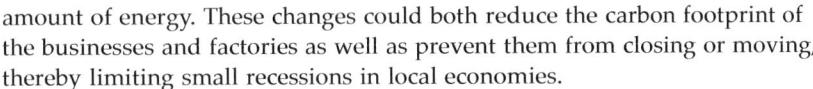

amount of energy. These changes could both reduce the carbon footprint of the businesses and factories as well as prevent them from closing or moving, thereby limiting small recessions in local economies.

The students in our schools are going to be the leaders of our next generation. It is our duty to provide them with the best possible learning environments so they can excel in schools in colleges, and in their lives. Pollutants released from factories and businesses near schools can be harmful to both the students and surrounding neighborhoods. For the benefit of our students, factories and businesses should be required to eliminate the harmful emission they release into the air. In our rapidly advancing world, it is likely new methods will be produced that eliminate pollution, and generate huge amounts of energy, but until that time is here, this is the best course of action to take.

Notice that Tyler doesn't take a position in the first paragraph. After establishing context with some broad brush strokes ("The world we live in is progressing at an exponential rate."), he simply parses the prompt and weaves back and forth between the various points of view, readying himself to provide his own perspective on the issue starting with his first body paragraph. In other words, he keeps his pencil moving and gets a lot of mileage out of the text so generously provided him by the ACT.

In the next two body paragraphs, he uses *perspective* to great advantage as both an organizing principle and as a transition between paragraphs. A nice touch stylistically and conceptually.

- **From a student's perspective . . .**
- **From a community perspective . . .**

In his third body paragraph (fourth paragraph overall), Tyler creates a *concession* paragraph, where he introduces the negative aspects that might accrue if businesses and factories had to relocate. But he softens the detrimental aspects of relocation by presenting positive changes that would actually help prevent businesses from closing. Another nice touch.

Finally, he wraps things up with a conclusion that simply summarizes the positions taken during his essay. A little flourish at the end — "In our rapidly advancing world" — gives his conclusion some sweep.

Throughout the essay, Tyler provided details, details, details and kept his pencil moving from one position to the next. Since word count — at least 450 words — is essential for a top-scoring ACT essay, these details allowed him to fill up almost three pages of lined space.

Finally, Tyler displays excellent narrative cohesion in his essay; his points flow logically one after the other, from his intro to conclusion, sweeping the reader along with them.

Summary — Tyler's T-charts

Here is how Tyler organized his arguments for this composition:

Pro	Con
Businesses and factories located near schools should be required to eliminate harmful pollutants. **Why** —	Businesses and factories located near schools should not be required to eliminate harmful pollutants. **Why** —

Sub-arguments

The health and safety of students and athletes is undermined by harmful emissions	Local economies would be hurt if businesses are forced to move
Community life would suffer from pollutants in the air	
Technology can provide solutions	

The following perspectives were employed:

Sub-argument	Perspective
Athletes need clean air to breath and students need to be healthy to stay ahead in school	From a student's perspective . . .
Community life would suffer and outdoor activities deterred	From a community perspective . . .

In his essay Tyler augmented his arguments with specific details, mentioning his water polo experiences in the bad air of Ontario, Sunday walks around the block for community members affected by pollution and technological advances such as solar panels and LEDs which might provide solutions to the problem of pollution.

In other words, Tyler fleshed out his essay with details, details, details.

ACT Prompt — June, 2013

Educators debate whether high school students should have an active role in classroom instruction, such as selecting some course materials and leading some class discussions. Some educators support giving students an active role in classroom instruction because they think doing so would increase students' interest in their classes. Other educators do not support giving students an active role in classroom instruction because they think students would not learn as much from their peers as they would from a teacher. In your opinion, should high school students have an active role in classroom instruction?

In your essay, take a position on this question. You may write about either one of the two points of view given, or you may present a different point of view on this question. Use specific reasons and examples to support your position.

In the previous chapter, I used this prompt to demonstrate a sample essay in order to outline some basic strategies for dealing with the prompt. Following is a real essay from Margot, another of my stellar students who does an excellent job.

Once again, the prompt provides you clear-cut pro and con positions on the topic, which you can cherry pick to get your essay started, which is exactly what Margo did, earning an almost perfect score.

Margot's Essay (score = 11)

In our current education system, what we as students learn in the classroom has little fluctuation. Students come to school expecting the same things every day, and the constant repetition can be boring and discourages the students from adventuring into and exploring their own ideas and interests. Students should be allowed to take an active role in classroom discussion. Although some educators may believe that too much diversity in curriculum of class would make learning standards unequal, to a great extent students taking an active role in classroom discussion would be beneficial because students would become more involved in classes, the teachers would have easier jobs and classes would become much more interesting.

From an academic perspective, allowing students to take an active role in classroom curriculum would encourage students to become more involved in their classes. If students were able to choose the curriculum that they wanted to learn in class, they would be much more interested and enthusiastic because they were able to decide what they were learning. Students would pick activities that they were passionate about and encourage other students

43

to get involved. In my US History Class, my teacher started a project where all students could write a play about any time period in US History that they wanted. Not only did I look forward to sharing my love and knowledge of the 1920s in class, but I also looked forward to that class period every day because I knew that something fun and exciting would be happening.

Furthermore, this new classroom set up would make it easier for the teachers. They would be able to relax and allow the students to run the class and therefore be rejuvenated for their times teaching in part of class. Teachers would also have more time to spend on lesson plans, which would enhance the students' learning experience. According to the New York Times, those teachers who spent just 30 minutes longer on their lesson plans had an increased student participation of 62%. Obviously, when teachers have more time, students get more out of the class.

However, some education officials believe that allowing students to take a greater role in leading their classes would give some students an advantage over others in standardized testing, or cause standardized testing scores to drop. However, an article from the Wall Street Journal showed that classes where there is higher student participation leads to higher test scores. And as I have shown with a New York Times article, classroom participation has risen as a result of students taking part in curriculum that they learn.

Another example that proves that allowing students to play a larger role in the classroom is that classes would be much more interesting and have much more variety. Students choosing what they want to learn will bring out the diverse interests of everyone in the classroom. They will be able to share their ideas and express their feelings bringing the class together as a whole. The class will become close and bond, fostering good relations outside of the classroom as well. More variety in the classroom would also encourage students to come to class more. According to the Washington Post which did a study on high school drop outs and why they chose to drop out showed that most high school dropouts left because they didn't feel wanted or because they were not interested in the curriculum and felt that they were not learning. If students were given a greater role in the classroom all of these problems would be solved. The high school dropout rates would decrease and this would benefit the school.

This leads me to my final point that the school would benefit. The new style of classes and its effectiveness would spread and more people would choose to apply to that school. **From a financial perspective**, increases in class size would result in greater funding for schools. Also, the school would benefit from happier students, decreasing bullying rates and fighting at school. Students would achieve higher test scores too, increasing school funding and prestige.

> In conclusion, we can see that students having a more active role in the classroom would do nothing but good for the students and the school as a whole. Bullying would decrease, standardized test scores would go up and the number of high school drop outs would decrease to name a few. For these reasons students should be given the opportunity to participate in the classroom. Not only would the students benefit, but the school as a whole would do well.

Like Tyler in the previous essay, Margot has simply parsed the prompt into pro and con positions, a convenient way to get the ball rolling on her composition. I can't stress enough how easy this approach makes ACT essay writing. Most writers fear the blank page. Some freeze, some faint, some run screaming from the test center. Just kidding.

But the simple truth is: once you understand that your intro paragraph is just a rehash of various statements served up to you on a silver platter in the prompt, augmented by your own opinions, the essay is a much less daunting proposition — in fact, getting started is a piece of cake.

Margot does all that, not only getting started quickly but also, unlike Tyler, throwing in her own opinion in the introduction, proposing that students should take an active role in their own education. Which is fine. It's up to you to decide how soon you want to take a position on the prompt. Use your T-chart as a guide.

Once Margot has the intro out of the way, she uses personal experience to support her position. Citing work done in her US History class, she's able to add compelling details to the narrative that make the writing flow smoothly and seem more relevant. Margot finishes up this paragraph in the first person, using "I", which is perfectly acceptable. Don't be afraid to use sentences that start "I look forward to . . . " or "I knew . . . " or "I believe . . ." After all, as we've seen, the ACT essay is simply a matter of opinion.

Notice, in particular, Margot's use of transitions (*furthermore* and *however*) in the next two body paragraphs: As mentioned in chapter 2, transitions are the mark of a skilled writer since they help the reader see where your narrative is going (*furthermore*) and when you plan to backtrack (*however*).

Also note that Margot brings in some external evidence to support her cause in the form of a New York Times article. In subsequent paragraphs, she references both the Wall Street Journal and the Washington Post. These newspapers are among the most widely respected in America and lend objective media credence to her arguments.

One minor nit: in the middle of her fourth paragraph, Margot veers slightly off course when she says, "However, an article in the Wall Street Journal showed that classes where there is higher student participation leads to higher test scores." Since this Journal reference actually supports her argument, a better transition would have been "*In fact,* an article in the Wall Street Journal . . . ". This just emphasizes how crucial transitions can be as directional signposts for the reader.

In her next-to-last body paragraph, Margot brings in school financing, using *perspective* as an embedded transition. Overall, she employed the following two perspectives/transitions to help support her essay:

- **From an academic perspective . . .**
- **From a financial perspective . . .**

Finally, her conclusion includes a broad summary of the positions taken during her essay. Throughout, Margot, like Tyler, provides details, details, details. Margot has well over 500 words to her credit and fills up over three pages of lined space.

Summary — Margot's T-charts

Here is how Margot organized her arguments for this composition:

Pro	Con
Student teachers should have an active role in the classroom **Why** —	Student teachers should not have an active role in the classroom **Why** —

Sub-arguments

Pro	Con
Students should explore their own interests to become more involved in classroom learning	Too much diversity in the classroom would make learning standards unequal
Student teachers foster an easy-going classroom atmosphere which helps reduce stress for teachers	
More variety in class means more students would attend	

The following perspectives were employed:

Sub-argument	Perspective
Students would become more involved in their classes and would learn more	From an academic perspective . . .
Increases in class size would result in more funding for school districts	From a financial perspective . . .

In her essay Margot augmented her arguments with specific details, mentioning how she wrote a play in her US History class, quoting the New York Times and Wall Street Journal, and bringing up issues such as increases in standardized test scores and decreases school bullying.

In other words, Margot, like Tyler, fleshed out her essay with details, details, details.

ACT Prompt — April, 2005

Foreign-language instruction is declining in public high schools in the US. Some people think this reflects the rise of English as the accepted language of commerce around the world and that knowledge of foreign languages is of lessening importance. Other people see the reduction in language study as a sign of the United States' failure to integrate with the rest of the world and a threat to the nation's vitality in an increasingly cross-cultural marketplace.

In your essay, take a position on this question. You may write about either one of the two points of view given, or you may present a different point of view on this question. Use specific reasons and examples to support your position.

Just to show that there's more than one way to approach an ACT essay, take a look at how Cessie handles this prompt in a practice essay, taking only a minimal swipe at the opposing viewpoint.

Cessie's Essay (score = 12)

While some individuals believe that English is the established language of commerce around the world and that knowledge of foreign languages is of lessening importance, the reduction in language study is actually a sign of the

United States' failure to integrate with the rest of the world and a threat to our nation's vitality in an increasingly cross-cultural marketplace. Studying foreign languages exposes students to different cultures, encouraging the tolerance and appreciation of others. Language study should be given greater support in American primary and secondary schools, as individuals will have the opportunity not only to broaden their knowledge and understanding of different cultures, but also to open doors to opportunities and jobs that are otherwise unattainable.

From a multi-cultural perspective, foreign languages, which expose individuals to different cultures and customs, are a sure remedy to the prejudice that our society holds against foreigners. With the popularity of television shows such as "Family Guy", which has long been criticized for its characters' racist remarks against African-Americans, the media imbues our citizens with the false notion that those of a different race are inherently inferior to white Americans. By exploiting the stereotypes of foreigners, the media abuses its position of influence and discourages tolerance in our society. Given the increasing accessibility of television and the internet, Americans can easily spread the notion that there is no one race, culture, or religion that is superior to another.

From an academic perspective, individuals learning multiple languages are better equipped to pursue diverse interests and professions. By overlooking or eliminating the importance of foreign language study, we are hindering our youth from maximizing their learning potential and opportunity to distinguish themselves in a highly competitive job market. Those who are raised in countries overseas that emphasize the study of multiple languages are not limited to professions in their homeland, and also have the opportunity to bring their strengths and cultural perspectives to other countries. If the United States does not encourage its citizens to expand their cultural knowledge, therefore limiting their ability to interact with other nations, America may not maintain its status as the leading economic power in the world.

A society that does not appreciate different cultures hinders its own ability to attain peace and balance. Commonly regarded as the "world's melting pot," America is comprised almost entirely of foreigners or descendants of immigrants. The amalgamation of these diverse individuals has earned America its reputation as the land of opportunity, in which an individual can rise from rags to riches regardless of his race. The very reason for founding America was for the sake of peace and freedom: to live life without oppression and without contempt. **From an egalitarian perspective**, our government, founded on a system of checks and balances, prevents any one entity from gaining too much power and functions similarly to a multicultural society that prevents the supremacy of any one race.

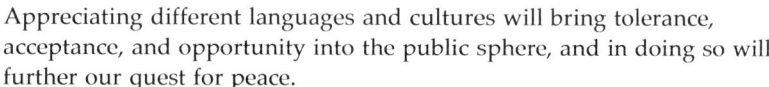

Appreciating different languages and cultures will bring tolerance, acceptance, and opportunity into the public sphere, and in doing so will further our quest for peace.

While the United States strives to maintain a peaceful and balanced society, this goal will only come to fruition if we choose to embrace foreign countries. As Americans, we should look to encourage the study of other languages just as many other nations have adopted the study of English. Ultimately, there are many benefits and lessons to learn from individuals who hail from different cultures, perspectives, and walks of life.

Cessie, a terrific and innovative writer with excellent narrative flow, gets off to a great start by quickly summarizing one side of the prompt (foreign language is of lessening importance) only to demolish it in the rest of her intro — and essay — citing the positive impact of foreign language learning in culture, jobs and the nation's vitality.

This is an interesting alternative strategy to ACT essay writing since it avoids the usual *concession paragraph* and makes a straight-up case for cultural integration via foreign language instruction. Which just goes to show that there is more than one way to compose an ACT essay. If you've got passionate arguments for one side of the prompt over the other, feel free to put all your energy into the side you want to represent, dismissing the opposition with a few opening salvos.

Note: Cessie isn't the only one who varied her ACT essay approach. To see how some of my students used SAT techniques to handle ACT prompts, see chapter 5 "Converting SAT Essays".

But back to Cessie's essay for a moment. Notice how she uses perspectives/transitions as openings for her first and second body paragraphs and embeds a transition in her third body paragraph. For example:

- From a multi-cultural perspective . . .
- From an academic perspective . . .
- From an egalitarian perspective . . .

Along with perspective/transitions, Cessie makes extensive use of subordination throughout her essay. As we've seen previously, subordination — or sentence variety — is one of the keys to good writing. To reinforce this point, let's take a look at some of the subordinate phrases and clauses (in italics) in Cessie's essay:

- *While some individuals believe that English is the established language of commerce around the world and that knowledge of foreign languages is of lessening importance*, the reduction in language study is actually a sign of the United States' failure to integrate with the rest of the world and a threat to our nation's vitality in an increasingly cross-cultural marketplace.

- Studying foreign languages exposes students to different cultures, *encouraging the tolerance and appreciation of others.*
- *Given the increasing accessibility of television and the internet,* Americans can easily spread the notion that there is no one race, culture, or religion that is superior to another.
- *By overlooking or eliminating the importance of foreign language study,* we are hindering our youth from maximizing their learning potential and opportunity to distinguish themselves in a highly competitive job market. Given the increasing accessibility of television and the internet, . . .

The moral of this story is this: sentence variety — subordination — plays a key part in top-scoring essays, in particular, and good writing in general. The more subordination, the better the prose . . . the better the prose, the higher the score.

Summary — Cessie's T-charts

Here is how Cessie organized her arguments for this composition:

Pro	Con
Foreign language instruction should be encouraged in high school. **Why** —	Foreign language instruction should not be encouraged in high school. **Why** —
Sub-arguments	
Foreign language study helps reduce stereotypes and exposes individuals to different cultures	— no arguments against
	Cessie's essay is the exception that proves the rule.
Foreign language study in school creates job opportunities	
	Unlike previous writers, Cessie eschews the use of a concession paragraph in her essay. She simply dismisses the opposition with the first sentence in her introduction and then lays out all the "pro" arguments for studying a foreign language in the remainder of her essay.
Encourages tolerance and enhances democratic principles	

The following perspectives were employed:

Sub-argument	Perspective
Students exposed to different cultures	From a multi-cultural perspective . .
Opens opportunities in highly competitive job markets	From an academic perspective . . .
Encourages tolerance and enhances democratic principles	From an egalitarian perspective . . .

In her essay Cessie augmented her arguments with specific details, mentioning popular TV shows like "Family Guy", discussing job markets overseas, referencing the "world's melting pot", and arguing for a democratic society with acceptance and opportunity for all. Lots of details, details, details.

ACT Prompt — June, 2005

In some high schools, students are required to complete a certain number of community service hours prior to graduation. Some people think community service is a good requirement because they think students will benefit from this experience. Other people think schools should not require community service because students will resent the requirement and, as a result, will not benefit from the experience. In your opinion, should high schools require students to complete a certain number of hours of community service?

In your essay, take a position on this question. You may write about either one of the two points of view given, or you may present a different point of view on this question. Use specific reasons and examples to support your position.

In the following essay, Bailey uses arguments from a variety of perspectives to buttress her position against mandatory community service.

Bailey's Essay (score = 11)

As students make their way through high school, they are often required to do certain things in order to graduate. For example, students are required to attend a specific set of history or mathematics classes. Requirements in regard to courses needed to graduate are usually not a controversial topic. However, there is much disagreement among schools in a different field: community service. In some high schools, students are required to complete a certain number of community service hours prior to graduation. Educators think that students will benefit from this experience and that communities will be enriched. Although this may seem like a good idea because it could hypothetically improve the town one lives in, in reality, it has a completely negative effect on students. I believe that if students are required to complete a minimum amount of community service, they will end up resenting the requirement.

One of the few arguments that supports required community service is the idea that students working a minimum amount of hours doing community service will benefit from this experience. **From a psychological perspective**, the good feeling that results from helping others could benefit a student's sense of self esteem. However, this feeling is not guaranteed due to the fact that students are being forced to complete hours, and may not want to even be helping anyone at all. The idea that community service improves a town is legitimate, but do people really want teenagers only helping out the community because they are required to do so for graduation? Obviously not. Forcing students to be "do-gooders" is in fact counterproductive. You can't legislate morality.

From an altruistic perspective, students who are forced to complete community service in order to graduate will not be volunteering out of the goodness of their hearts. The whole point of serving food at a homeless shelter or helping out at a church carnival in your town is because you genuinely want to be there and you thoroughly enjoy serving your community. When students choose to volunteer somewhere, their attitudes are positive, energetic, and happy, because they aren't being forced by their school to do something. In contrast, if they are simply showing up to serve food at a homeless shelter with a sour look on their face and an unfriendly personality, no one in the community will benefit because negative impressions will be passed from the students to the shelter occupants and all the way to the townspeople.

Finally, students are simply far too busy to add another task to their plate. With homework, after-school sports, tests such as the SAT and ACT, college applications, and so much more, students would surely crumble under the stress of having an additional requirement like community service. With so many things to do at once, students cannot put their whole effort into each area. Unfortunately, **from a practical standpoint**, he or she must choose which tasks are going to be a top priority, and excel at those few. With that being said, if students can't focus completely on their community service task, there is really no point in volunteering because chances are, with all the other things on their mind, they wouldn't do their best work.

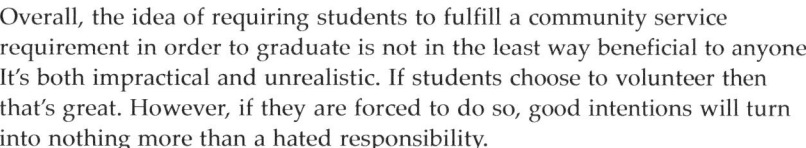

Overall, the idea of requiring students to fulfill a community service requirement in order to graduate is not in the least way beneficial to anyone. It's both impractical and unrealistic. If students choose to volunteer then that's great. However, if they are forced to do so, good intentions will turn into nothing more than a hated responsibility.

Summary — Bailey's T-charts

Here is how Bailey organized her arguments for this composition:

Pro	Con
Students should complete a certain number of community service hours in order to graduate. **Why** —	Students should not be forced to complete community service requirements in order to graduate. **Why** —

Sub-arguments	
Communities would be enriched by the work done by students	Students are already too busy with schoolwork, making community service impractical
Students would benefit psychologically from community service by an increase in self-esteem	Imposing community service on students is bad psychology. Altruism has to come from the heart.

Bailey presents these arguments from the following perspectives:

Sub-argument	Perspective
Students would benefit from community service by an increase in self-esteem	From a psychological perspective . . .
Students are already too busy with schoolwork, making community service impractical	From a practical perspective . . .
Imposing community service on students is bad psychology. Volunteering has to come from the heart.	From an altruistic perspective . . .

Throughout her essay Bailey uses excellent transitions and subordination to construct her essay. Mark of a good writer. She also includes details, details, details; however, this may be too much of a good thing, since some of the details in the essay seem to overlap, lowering her score.

To close out this selection of "Real Essays", let's return to the opening prompt of this chapter for which Tyler received a perfect score. Since not everyone will be so fortunate, I want to present a more workmanlike essay that received a lesser — but still respectable — score on the same prompt. I'll repeat the prompt below.

ACT Prompt — April, 2013

Lawmakers debate whether businesses and factories located near schools should be required to eliminate the pollutants and harmful emissions they release into the air. Some lawmakers support such a requirement because they think schools' learning environment should include safe and healthy air for students to breathe. Other lawmakers do not support such a requirement because they think it would force businesses and factories located near schools to close or move, which could hurt local economies. In your opinion, should businesses and factories located near schools be required to eliminate the pollutants and harmful emissions they release into the air?

In your essay, take a position on this question. You may write about either one of the two points of view given, or you may present a different point of view on this question. Use specific reasons and examples to support your position.

Here's how Bradley approached this topic:

Bradley's Essay (score = 9)

An increase in industrial growth and urbanization has become a common situation for countless cities throughout the globe. Industries provide many benefits to local economies, however the drawbacks of industrial growth can sometimes outweigh the positives. A pressing issue regarding businesses and factories has become whether or not they should be legal when they are located near schools, and consequently, students and youth. Some people claim that industrialization near schools is unhealthy for people and the environment. Others protest that the stimulation of local economies due to an increase in factories outweighs the harm.

From a business perspective, creating factories around schools is necessary for many people. Factories provide jobs for thousands of people. If a business is located near a school, then factory workers may have convenient commutes to work if they are the parents of a student. Furthermore, businesses near schools provide services to countless students and families. For example, "First-Line clothing Company" is a San Francisco based clothing brand. Their factories are located in neighborhoods and many schools. Because First-Line is so close to many potential customers, they are able to sell their products for cheaper for local people. They cut out shipping costs and other transportation services, resulting in cheaper clothes for many locals.

From a personal perspective, industrialization near schools is not worth the consequences. As someone who suffers from migraines, I would not be able to withstand attending a school with smog and other pollutants lingering in the air. Although migraines are only a temporary symptom of air pollution, some long-term sicknesses can result from inhaling factory smoke. Emphysema is just one disease that can come from inhaling air pollution. Even though students would not see the immediate effects of a disease like this, death and other serious illnesses can plague people as they grow older.

From an environmental perspective, industrialization is the cause of countless pressing issues that can affect students in school. One of which is global warming. As pollution is given off from factories and businesses, the Earth gradually warms. This can cause students to feel uncomfortable when outside. A ramification of this warming could be an increase in sunburns. Essentially, the environmental impact of industrialization causes danger at school.

This essay is good on a number of fronts. Good transitions, good subordination throughout, and good details ("First-Line clothing Company"). However, there are three main problems with the essay that result in a less-than-double-digit score:

- Low word count — Bradley's essay has only 369 words. To obtain a top score on an ACT essay you should have at least 450 words. Not fair, not just, but that's the way the game is played. So man up and keep the pencil moving.

- No conclusion — This really hurt Bradley's score. His essay just stops abruptly without any attempt to tie up loose ends, of which there are several. Of course, Bradley planned to add a conclusion but he just ran out of time.

  Like a football team on the opponent's ten-yard line of a close game when time runs out — bummer. Be sure to watch the clock and squeeze in a conclusion before time is called. Remember, all you have to do in your conclusion is summarize the points you've made earlier. If possible, tie the whole thing up with a pretty blue bow.

- Narrative cohesion and logical flow — This also hurt Bradley's score, perhaps even more than the lack of a conclusion. While he composes good paragraphs pro and con, he fails to navigate smoothly between them.

  Recall that top scoring ACT essays meld diverse viewpoints together harmoniously so that a strong common thread runs throughout. Ironically, even though Bradley uses three distinct perspectives to organize his ideas, there is no interaction between perspectives, no stylistic thread that ties them together. It's as though the perspectives were simply stacked on top of each other with no apparent relationship, like separate containers on a cargo ship.

  In an ACT essay, the readers need to see how each of the pieces in the essay relate to one another as a whole. Although the essay details are good, the presentation logic is flawed. Bradley needed better transitions and cross-references within paragraphs to better manage the flow.

What's Next

In the following chapter, we'll take a different approach to the ACT essay. Several of my SAT students have actually used strategies from my SAT essay-writing classes, adapted for use on the ACT essay.

If you are familiar with such strategies — or if you've read my book "How to Write a Killer SAT Essay" — please read on to see how you can employ your SAT content examples when constructing an ACT essay.

6—Converting SAT Essays

For those of you who are new to the ACT game but experienced in constructing SAT essays, you'll be happy to know that you can apply some of the same principles of SAT writing to your ACT essay.

As I describe in my book, "How to Write a Killer SAT Essay", examples from history, literature, movies, trash novels, sports, music, art, technology and personal experience can be used as content examples to support any SAT prompt.

Students learn how to pre-fabricate these content examples and "spin" them to whatever prompt the College Board throws at them. If you're already familiar with SAT-essay techniques, either from my book, my classes or through some other test prep organization, you can employ the same strategies to create a respectable-scoring ACT essay.

If you need a quick brush-up, see my essay workshop FREE on youtube: www.youtube.com/tctutoring.

Here's how one of my students applied SAT techniques to one of the ACT prompts we've seen previously.

ACT Prompt—June, 2013

Educators debate whether high school students should have an active role in classroom instruction, such as selecting some course materials and leading some class discussions. Some educators support giving students an active role in classroom instruction because they think doing so would increase students' interest in their classes. Other educators do not support giving students an active role in classroom instruction because they think students would not learn as much from their peers as they would from a teacher. In your opinion, should high school students have an active role in classroom instruction?

In your essay, take a position on this question. You may write about either one of the two points of view given, or you may present a different point of view on this question. Use specific reasons and examples to support your position.

Joe's Essay (score = 10)

As the noted physicist Albert Einstein once stated, "Imagination is more important than knowledge. For knowledge is limited, whereas imagination embraces the entire world, stimulating progress, giving birth to evolution." In other words, creativity, a part of science, allows a person to think "outside the box" thus uncovering new paths and new types of knowledge. Mankind has depended on creativity to come up with new inventions and ideas which now help shape our world today. By having high school students actively involved in the classroom, they can be exposed to new thoughts that they never would have gotten if they didn't participate. The belief that creativity and participation are needed more than ever in today's school system is portrayed throughout technology and literature.

Participation can lead students into becoming more interested in classes because it stimulates their minds with new possible ideas. One example where participation is needed more than ever is shown in the Scientific Revolution. Around 1726, Newton observed an apple fall from a tree and came to the conclusion that the apple accelerated due to gravity. He wondered if the same concept would still apply if the apple tree was twice as high as the original one. Therefore, this soon led him to the idea that the force of gravity could possibly reach to the moon, causing the moon to orbit the earth. From Newton's orbital cannon theory, with the right velocity, the projectile would always fall in the gravitational field of Earth which proves that the Moon can orbit around the Earth due to the acceleration of gravity. Newton then concluded that any two objects exert a gravitational force on each other. Although he was persecuted because his theories contradicted those of Aristotle's, his creative thoughts were beneficial toward the world. Now, in high school classrooms around the world, Newton's revolutionary ideas of gravity and orbital motion are taught as basic principles of learning.

Another example of why participation is key for high schools students is shown through literature. In Orson Scott Card's novel, Ender's Game, mankind has hardly survived two wars against the alien species known as the Buggers. In order to prepare for a third war, talented children with creative ideas are taken to a Battle School where they are trained to become fleet commanders. The protagonist, Ender Wiggin, actively talks to his comrades to acquire new styles of fighting. Through this, he reveals his strategic ideas in the arts of war through difficult battles. He amazes some of the commanders as they have never witnessed such things before. Ender makes progress by helping other novices prepare for the third war by having them participating in discussions. Later on, a commander, Mazer gives Ender one last test where his fleet is outnumbered by the Buggers. However Ender ends up destroying the Buggers and their planet through a masterful plan. Not

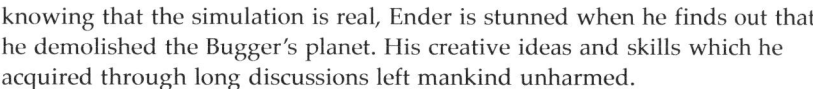

knowing that the simulation is real, Ender is stunned when he finds out that he demolished the Bugger's planet. His creative ideas and skills which he acquired through long discussions left mankind unharmed.

As these previous technological and literary examples have shown, there is a benefit in participating in school. High school students should be actively involved in every class so they can realize there are other ways to approach a question or a task. And this notion could possibly change our society into a thriving one. But this can't happen if we don't have everyone participate. As D. H. Lawrence once stated, "The ideas of one generation will become the instincts of the next."

Comments

Joe starts off his essay with typical SAT technique, quoting an important historical figure (Einstein) and making broad, sweeping statements in his introduction to establish context for the essay as a whole. His establishes creativity as the driving force for progress and then ties that into the prompt, saying:

> "By having high school students actively involved in the classroom, they can be exposed to new thoughts that they never would have gotten if they didn't participate."

Finally, Joe sums up his point of view and presents a roadmap to the readers that his essay will follow.

> The belief that creativity and participation are needed more than ever in today's school system is portrayed throughout technology and literature.

With technology as his first content example, Joe uses the Scientific Revolution as the mainstay of his first argument. More specifically, he charts the discoveries of Isaac Newton, from gravity to orbital cannon theory, supplying copious details along the way. Moreover, to demonstrate how new ideas are necessary to supplant old ideas, he contrasts Newton's work with that of Aristotle.

Finally, he ties Newton to the essay topic saying:

> Now, in high school classrooms around the world, Newton's revolutionary ideas of gravity and orbital motion are taught as basic principles of learning.

Some might argue that this content example is somewhat tangential to the prompt since it dwells more on history and science than participation of high school students in the classroom. In fact, this may account for Joe's score of 10, rather than 11 or 12, but my point here is that Joe is demonstrating significant conceptual and stylistic ability in this paragraph, sufficient to impress the readers and obtain a double-digit score. That puts him in the 90 percentile range among ACT essayists.

Joe's second content example is more directly correlated to the prompt since Ender Wiggin is directly responsible, as a student, for helping train his peers.

> The protagonist, Ender Wiggin, actively talks to his comrades to acquire new styles of fighting. Through this, he reveals his strategic ideas in the arts of war through difficult battles. He amazes some of the commanders as they have never witnessed such things before. Ender makes progress by helping other novices prepare for the third war by having them participating in discussions.

Throughout his essay, Joe uses extensive transitions and subordination (sentence variety) to guide the readers through the twists and turns in his essay. In the end, he wraps things up with a conclusion that emphasizes his main argument and finishes with a flourish, throwing in a quote from the great English writer, D. H. Lawrence.

Joe had used these two content examples (among others) in several SAT practice essays with me so he was well-armed with details, details, details and well-prepared to spin them to whatever ACT prompt came his way.

Here's another ACT essay which one of my students handled by converting her SAT content examples into an ACT essay.

ACT Prompt — June, 2005

> Some high schools in the United States have considered creating separate classrooms for male and female students in subjects such as mathematics and science. Some educators think separate classes will be beneficial because students will be less distracted from learning. Other educators think having separate classes for females and males will not be beneficial because it will seem to support stereotypes about differences in ability between males and females. In your opinion, should high schools create separate classes for male and female students?

> In your essay, take a position on this question. You may write about either one of the two points of view given, or you may present a different point of view on this question. Use specific reasons and examples to support your position.

Mariel's Essay (score = 12)

> As Elizabeth Cady Stanton, the famous abolitionist, women's suffragist, and author of The Woman's Bible, once said, "It is impossible for separation to lead to equality, for separation is discrimination and that is the worst form of evil." Clearly, Elizabeth Cady Stanton understood, as people today must now come to realize, that the struggle for gender equality has been an enduring

issue since the beginning of humanity. Women, especially over the course of the 19th and 20th centuries, have taken monumental strides in their fight for equal rights. However, this impending controversy of creating "separate classrooms" according to gender, threatens the equality that all women and girls rightly deserve. While some administrators believe that creating separate classes will be beneficial as students will be less distracted from learning, others believe that this separation will only serve to further support stereotypes about differences of ability between the genders. I firmly believe that the creation of separate classes will be detrimental not only to high school students, but also to their learning experience.

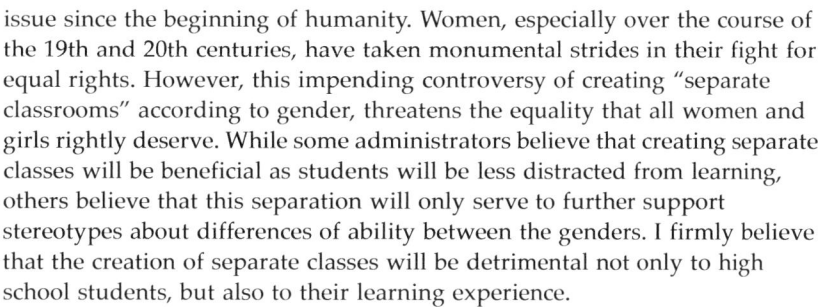

From a civil rights perspective, this action directly violates the women's rights and feminism movements that evolved throughout the late 1800s and 1900s. In the mid 1850s, women not only in the U.S. but also worldwide were consistently held to lower lower intellectual and physical standards than men as they were confined to their "sphere of domesticity" as homemakers. However, as the end of the century drew to a close, women began to be politically active, as they became the most dedicated abolitionists in the push for African American freedom. After seeing how much they accomplished, these activists soon turned into devout suffragists, which notably included Elizabeth Cady Stanton and Susan B. Anthony. Finally, in 1911, with decades of preserving effort in order to convince society that they were indeed capable and intellectual enough to vote, women gained this right with the 19th Amendment. This right, along with many others, were finally gained by the gender that had been oppressed throughout history. Separating classrooms would be a step backwards as it would encourage a stereotype of intellectual inferiority that has almost completely disappeared.

French physicist and chemist Marie Curie stands out as one of the great female scientists of all time. **From a technological perspective**, her entire life and career demonstrates that men and women scientists need to collaborate in intellectual environments in order to achieve significant progress. From the moment she began working in the scientific field, men constantly surrounded her. As she was the first female scientist in her department at the University of Paris at the turn of the 19th century, all of her collaborators were male associates. Luckily, they took her seriously and shared ideas on topics such as radioactivity. Marie Curie even worked closely with her husband Pierre Curie. All of this collaboration allowed her to pioneer research in radioactivity and discover Polonium and Radium, two previously unknown elements. Her discoveries have paved the way for the scientific advancements of modern society. Had she not had the opportunity to collaborate with men, there is no certainty that she would have made any of her notable discoveries. It would be unfortunate if educators took away this privilege from students who could largely benefit from comparing ideas and working with colleagues of both genders.

In conclusion, the separation of classrooms according to gender would be harmful not only to the students' social development and learning potential but also to their potential future success. Although some believe that this segregation will indeed lead to decreased distractions and promote a more focused environment, it is more evident that collaboration among students of opposing genders would be much more beneficial. This segregation could also encourage the stereotypical view of women as inferior to flourish and could keep all students from achieving their full potential. Society has achieved significant progress throughout the last century due largely to the fact that schools have been coeducational. Without this cohesion, humankind would have not been as progressive or achieved as much success.

Comments

Notice how Mariel blends SAT and ACT techniques. She starts out with typical SAT technique quoting a famous figure, in this case Elizabeth Cady Stanton. She then ties Stanton to the Women's movement, making the case for gender equality, which leads directly to a discussion of education equality and segregation in the classroom.

Having established context, Mariel moves into ACT gear, weaving between pro and con positions from the prompt. She concludes by taking a strong position:

> I firmly believe that the creation of separate classes will be detrimental not only to high school students, but also to their learning experience.

In her first body paragraph, she returns to Elizabeth Cady Stanton, placing her in the broad context of both Civil Rights and Women's Rights, concluding with an SAT-style reference to the 19th Amendment. In this paragraph, Mariel makes a broad-based and compelling argument that separating males and females in the classroom would "be a step backwards as it would encourage a stereotype of intellectual inferiority that has almost completely disappeared."

In her second body paragraph, Mariel introduces Marie Curie and makes the case that collaboration with the opposite sex benefits both men and women.

> Had she not had the opportunity to collaborate with men, there is no certainty that she would have made any of her notable discoveries. It would be unfortunate if educators took away this privilege from students who could largely benefit from comparing ideas and working with colleagues of both genders..

Both of these paragraphs are framed with the following perspectives:

* From a civil rights perspective, . . .
* From a technological perspective, . . .

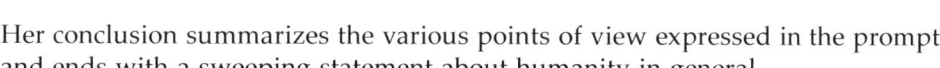

Her conclusion summarizes the various points of view expressed in the prompt and ends with a sweeping statement about humanity in general.

> Without this cohesion, humankind would have not been as progressive or achieved as much success.

Like Joe in the previous essay, Mariel uses extensive transitions and subordination to guide the readers through the twists and turns in this essay.

Joe and Mariel demonstrate that, with a little creativity, ACT prompts can be addressed with hybrid techniques that blend both SAT and ACT strategies.

SAT vs ACT Prompts — Summary

Because the SAT is a national test, the prompts are generic, involving issues that lend themselves to different — and invariably conflicting — points of view. The easiest way to address such issues is to emphasize the dramatic elements inherent in the subject matter. As a result, regardless of the wording, all SAT prompts can be boiled down to themes involving one word: **drama**.

No matter what the SAT prompt *appears* to say, you can address it using prefabricated content examples that interweave three basic motifs:

- Overcoming obstacles
- Meeting challenges
- Achieving progress — either individual, social or both

ACT prompts are also generic and involve conflicting points of view but they have a significant emphasis — they all deal with someone in a position of authority (teachers, administrators, officials) attempting to control or restrict some school-related activity of teenagers.

While ACT prompts are local, micro-based prompts, SAT prompts are broad, macro-based prompts. Nonetheless, as we have seen, content examples from history, literature, technology, pop culture and science can also be successfully applied to ACT essays.

To demonstrate this in action, I'll conclude this chapter with a series of paragraphs drawn from my SAT student essays and applied to abbreviated ACT prompts. This, along with the full-length essays presented earlier in this chapter, should give you a jump-start on utilizing your own SAT-style content to dominate the ACT essay.

Converting SAT Content

- *ACT prompt:* Should greater support be given to foreign language programs in high schools in the United States?

Here's how one of my students converted her SAT paragraph on John Adams to fit this ACT prompt:

> *SAT response:* Foreign language study is essential for a well-rounded and progressive education and should be required of all high school students. This is exemplified by president John Adam's trip to France in 1773. The United States was losing their battle for independence from Britain and the military needed the support of any who could help. In a desperate, and what many deemed "hopeless", attempt to gain a powerful ally, Adams sailed to France to meet with Benjamin Franklin and Arthur Lee, where they hoped to forge an alliance with France. Adams immersed himself in French culture, attending the theatre, and befriending many dignitaries. Eventually, he met with 24 year old, Louis XIV who, after much persuasion, agreed to form an alliance. If John Adams had not been required to learn French in school and been willing to travel to a foreign country, the United States may not have won their independence from Britain. Therefore, foreign languages should be a requirement in high school.

- *ACT prompt:* Should high schools require students to complete a certain number of hours of community service?

Here's how another students converted a personal experience content example from one of her SAT essays to fit this ACT prompt:

> *SAT response*: Community service cannot be mandated from above by high school officials. It should come from the heart in response to serious and catastrophic events. A few years ago I traveled to New Orleans to help with the Hurricane Katrina relief effort. No one told me I had to volunteer for this effort. I just felt it was the right thing to do. I remember mentally preparing myself by imagining a city so broken down that it would take years to fix. Yet, when I actually arrived in New Orleans, I realized that none of the images I had created in my mind came close to the horror that was laid out in front of me. During my two weeks in New Orleans, I had to brainstorm with others ways to rescue people out of teeny crevices and think of words that would make terrified people feel at ease. I learned that in any situation where people are scared out of their minds, individuals who care can make a real difference. Students forced into community service would not have the right attitude to truly care for the sick and injured.

- *ACT prompt:* Should businesses and factories located near schools be required to eliminate the pollutants and harmful emissions they release into the air?

In this converted SAT content example, the Chernobyl disaster is creatively spun to support arguments against pollution:

SAT response: Not only should business be required to eliminate pollutants and harmful emissions into the air, they shouldn't be allowed to be built next to schools in the first place. Let me take an extreme example from Russia to make my point. During the early 1980's technological advancements there set nuclear power on the fast track to success. Yet, for all the scientific progress made in the field to keep nuclear power safe, in 1986 the power plant in Chernobyl, Ukraine exploded. A series of operator actions, including the disabling of automatic shutdown mechanisms led to the release of deadly fission products into the atmosphere. This left hundreds dead and caused severe fallout all over the city. Imagine the death toll if this nuclear power plant had been built next to schools crowded with children and teenagers. Of course, this example is exaggerated but the idea of school children exposed to any sort of pollution cannot be tolerated.

- *ACT prompt:* Should a police patrol officer be assigned to public high schools?

An obvious response to this ACT prompt is to reference 1984, as the following converted SAT content example demonstrates:

SAT response: I dread the day we see police officers prowling the halls of our local high schools. In George Orwell's famous novel, everyone is being watched and controlled by Big Brother. Big Brother's government is very oppressive and tries to eliminate all chances of rebellion. They are even creating a new language called newspeak that eliminates all words that could threaten the government's power. The main character, Winston Smith, starts to resent Big Brother and he starts to rebel by writing in a diary and getting a girlfriend. These actions would not be looked down upon in the real world, but in this novel they are very illegal. Eventually, Winston gets caught doing these very illegal things and is taught to love Big Brother again. This form of totalitarian society prohibits humans from any kind of individuality or freedom. Do we really want to see democracy destroyed like this? A police officer patrolling the halls of my high school is the first step toward Orwell's 1984 vision of government oppression.

- *ACT prompt:* Should more elective courses like music and art be provided in high schools?

This ACT prompt is easily handled with an SAT style paragraph on artists like Picasso, Da Vinci or Andy Warhol:

SAT response: Previous to the nineteen sixties, art was considered to reflect emotion, knowledge and beauty. Andy Warhol, however, chose to redefine art by "thinking outside the box". Andy Warhol, an enigmatic artist during the sixties and seventies influenced artists around the world to create a new style of art, Pop Art. Warhol advanced the idea of art by creating a new artistic twist by using vibrant colors, and familiar objects and celebrities as his subject. His portrait of Marilyn Monroe is praised by fans everywhere. If Andy Warhol had not been allowed to pursue his passion for art in high school, perhaps he would not have become the artist we know today. Providing an outlet for promising artists in high school is an excellent way to produce more artists of Warhol's stature. In my opinion, elective courses should be retained in high school. The availability of such courses give potential artists, whether in art, music or drama, a creative means for expression which enriches society in the long run.

7—Your Turn

A good way to ensure that you've assimilated all the information in this book is to sit down and write a couple of practice ACT essays. I'll include some prompts we've seen in earlier chapters, as well as empty T-charts so you can organize your thoughts "pro" and "con" in preparation for your essay. Time yourself and try to spend no more than three minutes gathering your thoughts.

Then start writing on the lined paper provided for the remaining 27 minutes. Your goal is to include at least 450 words for a top-scoring essay. If you can't reach the 450 word limit the first time out, keep trying until you do. Remember, the essay is all about your opinions and perspectives, expressed in elegant prose and buttressed with as many details, details, details as humanly possible in each body paragraph.

In your conclusion just wrap up and summarize everything you've written about. If possible, add a little contextual flourish at the end — a quote, an interesting observation, an anecdote or a personal reflection.

Once you've successfully covered the essay prompts in this chapter, search the net for other ACT prompts and keep working, keep practicing.

Here's a recent prompt, one we saw in chapter 4, "Sample Essay". Now you try it on your own. You can always refer back to the sample essay when you're done to compare your work.

ACT Prompt — Practice 1

Educators debate whether high school students should have an active role in classroom instruction, such as selecting some course materials and leading some class discussions. Some educators support giving students an active role in classroom instruction because they think doing so would increase students' interest in their classes. Other educators do not support giving students an active role in classroom instruction because they think students would not learn as much from their peers as they would from a teacher. In your opinion, should high school students have an active role in classroom instruction?

In your essay, take a position on this question. You may write about either one of the two points of view given, or you may present a different point of view on this question. Use specific reasons and examples to support your position.

Here's a T-chart to get you started. First parse the prompt into "pro" and "con" positions, then generate sub-arguments based on your opinions.

Pro	Con

Sub-arguments

Now connect your sub-arguments with a few perspectives:

Sub-argument	Perspective
	From a . . . perspective . . .
	From a . . . perspective . . .
	From a . . . perspective . . .

Armed with a solid roadmap of where you're going and what you're arguing for and against, put pen to paper and get busy!

Note: Three pages of lined space are provided below with approximately 80 lines. The horizontal length of the lines on the actual ACT test is a little longer than the lines on these pages. However, writing 6 words per line here x 75 lines gets you to the desired 450 word count. Strive for that number.

ACT Prompt — Practice 2

In some states, legislators have debated whether teenagers should be required to maintain a "C" grade average in school before receiving a driver's license. Some people think this would be a good policy because having passing grades shows that students are responsible enough to be good drivers. Other people think such a policy would not be appropriate because they see no relationship between grades in school and driving skills. In your opinion, should teenagers be required to maintain a "C" average in school before receiving a driver's license?

In your essay, take a position on this question. You may write about either one of the two points of view given, or you may present a different point of view on this question. Use specific reasons and examples to support your position?

Here's another T-chart to fill in. As previously, parse the prompt into "pro" and "con" positions, then generate sub-arguments based on your opinions.

Pro	Con
Sub-arguments	

Now connect your sub-arguments with a few perspectives:

Sub-argument	Perspective
	From a . . . perspective . . . From a . . . perspective . . . From a . . . perspective . . .

If you need help determining your positions and perspectives on this prompt — or reinforcement of your approach — feel free to refer back to Chapter 4 "Sample Essay" for help. The last essay in the chapter breaks down this prompt.

If you feel confident in your analysis, then get going with your essay.

_____

_____

_____

_____

_____

_____

_____

_____

_____

_____

_____

_____

_____

_____

_____

_____

_____

75

ACT Prompt — Practice 3

Educators debate extending high school to five years because of increasing demands on students from employers and colleges to participate in extracurricular activities and community service in addition to having high grades. Some educators support extending high school to five years because they think students need more time to achieve all that is expected of them. Other educators do not support extending high school to five years because they think students would lose interest in school and attendance would drop in the fifth year. In your opinion, should high school be extended to five years?

In your essay, take a position on this question. You may write about either one of the two points of view given, or you may present a different point of view on this question. Use specific reasons and examples to support your position.

Here's another T-chart to fill in. Parse the prompt into "pro" and "con" positions, then generate sub-arguments based on your opinions.

Pro	Con
Sub-arguments	

Now connect your sub-arguments with a few perspectives:

Sub-argument	Perspective
	From a . . . perspective . . . From a . . . perspective . . . From a . . . perspective . . .

You're on your own with this prompt. But by now you should feel confident in your ability to produce a lengthy, well-constructed, top-scoring ACT essay. Good luck!

_____

_____

_____

_____

_____

_____

_____

_____

_____

_____

_____

_____

_____

_____

_____

_____

_____

_____

Parting Thoughts

Just so you know, further help is on the way. This summer I'll distribute a comprehensive and FREE youtube workshop covering the essentials of ACT essay writing.

At present, for SAT students, I have a free eleven-part youtube presentation entitled "Killer SAT Essay Workshop". You can access it at:

www.yotube.com/tctutoring

My upcoming "Killer ACT Essay Workshop" on youtube will follow the methodology presented in this book.

In addition, for students with iPhones, my "Killer SAT Grammar" app is available **FREE** at the App Store. While the ACT grammar format differs from that of the SAT, the grammar points covered in this app are generic enough to be of value to ACT students as well. Here's the link:

www.satgrammarapp.com

Finally, in case you want to visit, here's my website:

www.tctutoring.net

Good luck with your essay, with college, with life!

Made in the USA
Lexington, KY
11 June 2015